Fredrick Wonders

# How To Set Trends On All Social Media Platforms

*Mastering Strategies For Setting Trends And Influence On Social Media*

*First published by Fredrick Wonders 2024*

*Copyright © 2024 by Fredrick Wonders*

*All rights reserved. No part of this publication may be reproduced, stored or transmitted in any form or by any means, electronic, mechanical, photocopying, recording, scanning, or otherwise without written permission from the publisher. It is illegal to copy this book, post it to a website, or distribute it by any other means without permission.*

*First edition*

*This book was professionally typeset on Reedsy*
*Find out more at reedsy.com*

*To all those who dare to innovate, create, and inspire on the ever-evolving canvas of social media. Your passion drives change and shapes the digital landscape.*

*Warm regards,*

*Fredrick Wonders*

"Empower your brand. Lead trends. Master social media."

                                        Fredrick Wonders

# Contents

Foreword ................................................................. 1
Preface .................................................................... 5
Acknowledgement ................................................... 8
1. Introduction to Trendsetting ............................... 10
2. Understanding Social Media Platforms ............ 15
3. Analyzing Current Trends ................................. 23
4. Creating Trend-Worthy Content ........................ 29
5. Leveraging Influencers and Partnerships ......... 37
6. Utilizing Hashtags and Trends .......................... 44
7. Engaging with Your Audience .......................... 51
8. Analyzing and Adapting Your Strategy ............ 58
9. Creating Viral Content ...................................... 66
10. Leveraging Influencers and Partnerships ....... 74
11. Harnessing the Power of Paid Advertising .... 83
12. Building a Community and Engaging with Your Audience ................................................................ 93
    1.
    2.
    3.
    4.
    5.

6.
7.
8.
9.
10.
11.
12.
13.
14.

# Foreword

Foreword

In the early days of social media, platforms like Facebook, Twitter, and YouTube were seen as casual spaces for personal expression and connection. Fast forward to today, and these platforms have transformed into powerful engines of influence, driving global conversations, shaping public opinion, and impacting virtually every industry. The ability to set trends on social media has become a highly sought-after skill, one that can propel brands to new heights and create cultural phenomena overnight.

"Setting Trends on Social Media: A Blueprint for Success" is a timely and indispensable guide for anyone looking to navigate this complex and ever-changing landscape. As someone who has been deeply immersed in the world of digital marketing and social media strategy for over a decade, I can attest to the profound impact that a well-executed social media strategy can have on a brand's success. The insights, tools, and strategies shared in this book are the result of extensive research, practical experience, and a deep understanding of what makes social media tick.

What sets this book apart is its holistic approach. It doesn't just focus on the technical aspects of social media marketing, such as data analytics and paid advertising; it also delves into the art of storytelling, the importance of authenticity, and the power of community building. These elements are crucial for creating a lasting impact and driving meaningful engagement. By combining these aspects with actionable advice and real-world case studies, this book provides a comprehensive roadmap for setting trends and achieving success on social media.

One of the most valuable aspects of this book is its emphasis on authenticity. In an age where consumers are increasingly skeptical of traditional advertising and promotional tactics, authenticity has emerged as a key differentiator. Audiences crave genuine connections and meaningful interactions with brands. They want to see the human side of businesses and engage with content that resonates on a personal level. This book provides practical guidance on how to build and maintain these authentic connections, ensuring that your social media efforts are not just effective but also sustainable.

Another strength of this book is its focus on community building. Social media is inherently social, and the most successful brands are those that cultivate vibrant, engaged communities around their content. Whether you're an entrepreneur looking to build a loyal customer base, a marketer aiming to drive brand awareness, or an influencer seeking to expand your reach, the strategies outlined in this book will help you create and nurture a thriving community.

As you read through the chapters, you'll discover a wealth of knowledge that will empower you to harness the full potential of social media. You'll learn how to create compelling content, leverage data to inform your strategy, engage with your audience authentically, and ultimately, set trends that resonate and endure. This book is not just a guide; it's a blueprint for success in the dynamic world of social media.

I am confident that "Setting Trends on Social Media: A Blueprint for Success" will become an invaluable resource for anyone looking to make their mark in the digital space. The insights and strategies shared here are not just theoretical; they are tried and tested, proven to deliver results. Whether you're just starting your social media journey or looking to take your existing efforts to the next level, this book will provide the guidance and inspiration you need to succeed.

Here's to your journey of setting trends and making a lasting impact on social media.

Sincerely,

Fredrick                                                                 Wonders

# Preface

Preface: Setting Trends on Social Media - A Blueprint for Success

In today's digital age, social media is not just a platform for connection; it's a powerful tool for influence, business growth, and trendsetting. The landscape of social media is ever-evolving, with new platforms emerging, algorithms changing, and user behaviors shifting. Amidst this dynamic environment, one constant remains: the potential to create and set trends that captivate audiences worldwide.

"Setting Trends on Social Media: A Blueprint for Success" is a comprehensive guide designed to help you navigate the complexities of social media and harness its power to establish your brand as a trendsetter. Whether you're an entrepreneur, marketer, influencer, or simply someone passionate about digital media, this book provides the strategies, tools, and insights needed to make a significant impact.

Over the past decade, we've witnessed how viral content can elevate brands to new heights, how influencers can shift consumer behaviors, and how businesses can leverage social media to build loyal communities. From the overnight sensation of viral videos to meticulously crafted brand campaigns, the ability to set trends on social media has become a coveted skill. But what does it take to consistently create content that resonates, engages, and inspires?

In this book, we delve into the art and science of trendsetting on social media. We'll explore the foundational principles of crafting compelling content, the importance of storytelling, and the techniques for engaging with audiences authentically. We'll examine case studies of brands and influencers who have mastered the art of trendsetting, providing you with actionable insights and practical tips.

We'll also cover the technical aspects of social media marketing, including data analytics, platform algorithms, and paid advertising strategies. By understanding these elements, you can optimize your efforts, reach your target audience more effectively, and measure your success with precision.

Furthermore, this book emphasizes the human element of social media. Building a community, fostering relationships, and engaging with your audience authentically are critical components of setting trends. We'll guide you on how to create meaningful interactions that not only boost engagement but also build trust and loyalty.

As you embark on this journey through the chapters, remember that setting trends is not just about going viral or gaining followers. It's about creating a lasting impact, driving conversations, and shaping the culture within your niche. It's about understanding your audience, delivering value, and staying ahead of the curve.

This book is your blueprint for success in the fast-paced world of social media. Whether you're starting from scratch or looking to enhance your existing strategy, the insights and strategies shared here will equip you with the knowledge and confidence to set trends and achieve your social media goals.

Welcome to the exciting world of social media trendsetting. Let's get started on creating your blueprint for success.

Fredrick                                                                Wonders

# Acknowledgement

Acknowledgments

Writing a book on setting trends on social media has been a collaborative effort that would not have been possible without the support and contributions of many individuals and organizations. I would like to express my heartfelt gratitude to everyone who has played a role in bringing this project to fruition.

First and foremost, I am deeply grateful to [Your Company/Organization] for providing the resources, support, and encouragement needed to undertake this endeavor. Your commitment to innovation and excellence has been a constant source of inspiration.

I extend my sincere thanks to [Name], whose expertise and guidance have been invaluable throughout the writing process. Your insights and advice have helped shape the content of this book and have made it stronger.

I would also like to thank the numerous professionals, influencers, and industry experts who generously shared their experiences and insights. Your contributions have enriched the content of this book and have provided readers with practical, real-world perspectives on setting trends on social media.

To my family and friends, thank you for your unwavering support and understanding during late nights and weekends spent writing. Your encouragement has kept me motivated and focused.

Last but not least, I am grateful to the readers of this book. It is my sincere hope that the strategies, tools, and insights shared within these pages will empower you to succeed in setting trends on social media and achieving your goals.

Thank you all for being a part of this journey.

Warm regards,

Fredrick                                                    Wonders

# 1

# Introduction to Trendsetting

## Introduction to Trendsetting

### What is Trendsetting?

Trendsetting on social media involves creating and promoting content that captures the public's imagination, encourages engagement, and spreads virally across platforms. It's about being at the forefront of new ideas, styles, and conversations that resonate with a wide audience. Successful trendsetting can position you or your brand as a leader and influencer in your industry or niche.

### Why is Trendsetting Important?

1. Increased Visibility: Setting trends can significantly boost your visibility and reach. When your content goes viral, it

can be seen by millions of people worldwide, vastly expanding your audience.

2. Brand Authority: Being a trendsetter establishes you as an authority in your field. People look to trendsetters for the latest information, styles, and ideas, enhancing your credibility and influence.

3. Engagement and Loyalty: Trendsetting content often sparks conversation and engagement. This interaction builds a community around your brand and fosters loyalty among your followers.

4. Competitive Advantage: In a crowded digital landscape, setting trends can differentiate you from competitors. It positions you as an innovator and leader, making it easier to attract and retain followers.

## Key Elements of Trendsetting

1. Creativity: Trendsetting requires fresh, innovative ideas that stand out from the crowd. Whether it's a unique visual style, a compelling story, or a new way of engaging with your audience, creativity is essential.

2. Strategic Thinking: It's not enough to create great content; you need a strategy to promote and distribute it effectively. Understanding the algorithms, timing, and mechanics of each social media platform is crucial.

3. Understanding Your Audience: Knowing your audience's preferences, interests, and behaviors allows you to create content that resonates with them. Tailored content is more likely to be shared and go viral.

4. Consistency: Building a trend takes time and persistence. Consistently posting high-quality content keeps your audience engaged and increases your chances of setting a trend.

5. Engagement: Interacting with your audience helps build a community. Responding to comments, messages, and engaging in conversations makes your audience feel valued and more likely to support and share your content.

## The Trendsetting Process

1. Research and Analysis: Begin by researching current trends and analyzing what makes them successful. Use tools like Google Trends, social media analytics, and trend reports to understand what's popular and why.

2. Content Creation: Develop content that has the potential to become a trend. This could be a new challenge, a unique visual style, a catchy hashtag, or a viral video concept. Ensure your content is high-quality and engaging.

3. Promotion: Use various strategies to promote your content. Collaborate with influencers, use targeted advertising, and leverage multiple platforms to maximize reach.

4. Engagement and Interaction: Foster engagement by responding to comments, encouraging user-generated content, and participating in conversations. Engagement helps build a community and amplifies your content's reach.

5. Monitoring and Adjustment: Continuously monitor the performance of your content. Use analytics to track engagement, reach, and other key metrics. Be prepared to adjust your strategy based on what's working and what's not.

Trendsetting on social media is a dynamic and rewarding process. By combining creativity, strategic thinking, and a deep understanding of your audience, you can create content that not only captures attention but also spreads virally, establishing you as a leader in your field.

# 2

# Understanding Social Media Platforms

**Understanding Social Media Platforms**

Each social media platform has its unique characteristics, audience, and content formats. To set trends effectively, it's crucial to understand these differences and tailor your approach accordingly. This chapter provides an in-depth look at the major social media platforms and how to leverage them for trendsetting.

### Facebook

**Overview**

User Demographics: Broad age range, with significant usage among adults aged 25-54.

Content Types: Text posts, images, videos, live streams, stories, links.

Algorithm: Prioritizes content that generates meaningful interactions (comments, shares, reactions).

### Trendsetting Strategies

1. Create Engaging Posts: Use compelling visuals and storytelling to capture attention. Ask questions and encourage comments to boost interaction.

2. Leverage Facebook Groups: Create or join groups related to your niche. Engage with members and share valuable content to establish authority.

3. Utilize Facebook Live: Live streams tend to get higher engagement. Use them for Q&A sessions, product launches, or behind-the-scenes content.

4. Boost Posts: Use Facebook Ads to promote key content. Target specific demographics to maximize reach.

### Instagram

## Overview

User Demographics: Popular among younger audiences, especially 18-34-year-olds.

Content Types: Photos, videos, stories, IGTV, Reels.

Algorithm: Prioritizes engagement (likes, comments, shares), recency, and relationship with followers.

## Trendsetting Strategies

1. High-Quality Visuals: Invest in professional photography and editing. Aesthetic and cohesive feeds attract more followers.

2. Stories and Reels: Use Stories for daily updates and Reels for short, engaging videos. Participate in popular challenges to increase visibility.

3. Hashtags: Research and use relevant hashtags to reach a wider audience. Create a unique, branded hashtag to encourage user-generated content.

4. Collaborations: Partner with influencers and brands. Cross-promotions can help you tap into new audiences.

## Twitter

### Overview

User Demographics: Widely used by adults aged 18-49, with a focus on news, politics, and real-time events.

Content Types: Short text posts (tweets), images, videos, threads, polls.

Algorithm: Prioritizes recency, engagement (retweets, likes, replies), and content from followed accounts.

### Trendsetting Strategies

1. Real-Time Engagement: Tweet regularly about trending topics. Use relevant hashtags to join larger conversations.

2. Concise and Witty: Craft concise, witty tweets. Humor and relatability can increase the likelihood of retweets and shares.

3. Threads: Use threads to provide in-depth information. This format keeps followers engaged and encourages retweets.

4. Polls and Questions: Create polls and ask questions to foster interaction and gather insights from your audience.

## TikTok

### Overview

User Demographics: Predominantly used by younger audiences, especially teenagers and young adults.

Content Types: Short-form videos (15-60 seconds), duets, challenges.

Algorithm: Prioritizes engagement (likes, comments, shares), completion rate, and trending sounds.

### Trendsetting Strategies

1. Creative Content: Focus on creativity and authenticity. Unique and entertaining videos are more likely to go viral.

2.Participate in Challenges: Join popular challenges and create your own. Challenges can quickly gain traction if they resonate with users.

3. Use Trending Sounds: Incorporate trending music and sounds into your videos to increase discoverability.

4. Engage with Others: Collaborate with other TikTok users through duets and stitches. Engage with comments to build a community.

## YouTube

### Overview

User Demographics: Broad age range, with significant usage among 18-49-year-olds.

Content Types: Long-form videos, vlogs, tutorials, reviews, live streams, shorts.

Algorithm: Prioritizes watch time, engagement (likes, comments, shares), and subscriber activity.

### Trendsetting Strategies

1. Consistent Uploads: Maintain a regular upload schedule to keep your audience engaged.

2. High-Quality Production: Invest in good equipment and editing software. Professional-looking videos attract more viewers.

3. Optimize for Search: Use SEO techniques in your titles, descriptions, and tags. This helps your videos appear in search results.

4. Collaborations: Work with other YouTubers to reach new audiences. Collaborative videos often perform well due to cross-promotion.

## LinkedIn

### Overview

User Demographics: Primarily used by professionals, with a focus on B2B networking and industry-specific content.

Content Types: Articles, posts, videos, professional updates, job listings.

Algorithm: Prioritizes professional relevance, engagement (likes, comments, shares), and connections.

**Trendsetting Strategies**

1. Thought Leadership: Share industry insights, case studies, and professional advice. Establish yourself as an expert in your field.

2. Engage with Professionals: Comment on and share posts from others in your industry. Build a network of like-minded professionals.

3. Publish Articles: Write and publish long-form articles on LinkedIn to provide value and showcase your expertise.

4. Use Rich Media: Incorporate images, videos, and infographics in your posts to make them more engaging.

Understanding the unique characteristics and user demographics of each social media platform is essential for effective trendsetting. Tailor your content and strategies to fit the platform's strengths and audience preferences. By doing so, you increase your chances of setting trends and achieving viral success across multiple social media channels.

# 3

# Analyzing Current Trends

**Analyzing Current Trends**

To set trends effectively, you must first understand the landscape of current trends. This chapter delves into how to identify, analyze, and learn from existing trends to inform your own strategy.

**Understanding Trends**

A trend on social media is a pattern or movement in behavior that gains widespread popularity over time. Trends can manifest in various forms, such as hashtags, challenges, memes, topics, or specific types of content. Recognizing and analyzing these trends is crucial for staying relevant and proactive in your content creation.

## Identifying Trends

1. Social Media Monitoring Tools: Utilize tools like Hootsuite, Sprout Social, or Brandwatch to monitor trending topics, hashtags, and conversations. These tools provide real-time data on what's gaining traction across platforms.

2. Google Trends: Use Google Trends to see what people are searching for online. This tool shows the popularity of search queries over time, allowing you to identify emerging trends.

3. Explore Pages and Trending Sections: Regularly check the explore pages and trending sections of platforms like Instagram, Twitter, and TikTok. These sections highlight popular content and hashtags.

4. Industry Reports and News: Follow industry-specific reports and news outlets. These sources often highlight key trends and shifts within particular niches.

5. Competitor Analysis: Observe what your competitors are doing. Analyze their successful content and strategies to understand what's working in your industry.

## Analyzing Trends

Once you've identified potential trends, the next step is to analyze them to understand why they're successful and how you can leverage similar elements. Here are key factors to consider:

1. Engagement Levels: Look at the number of likes, comments, shares, and overall engagement a trend is generating. High engagement indicates a strong connection with the audience.

2. Audience Demographics: Understand who is engaging with the trend. Analyzing the age, gender, location, and interests of the audience helps tailor your content to similar demographics.

3. Content Format: Identify the type of content driving the trend. Is it videos, images, memes, or text posts? Knowing this helps you create content that fits the preferred format.

4. Emotional Appeal: Assess the emotional triggers behind the trend. Trends often resonate because they evoke strong emotions, whether it's humor, nostalgia, excitement, or empathy.

5. Timing and Context: Consider the timing and context in which the trend emerged. Is it tied to a specific event, season,

or cultural moment? Timing can play a crucial role in a trend's success.

## Learning from Trends

1. Adapt and Innovate: While it's important to understand existing trends, don't just replicate them. Adapt the elements that work and innovate to bring a fresh perspective. Originality is key to standing out.

2. Audience Insights: Use trends to gain insights into your audience's preferences and behaviors. What types of content are they drawn to? What topics do they care about? Use this information to refine your strategy.

3. Content Strategy: Incorporate trending elements into your content strategy. This could mean participating in popular challenges, using trending hashtags, or adopting new content formats that are gaining traction.

4. Test and Iterate: Experiment with different types of content and measure their performance. Use A/B testing to see what resonates best with your audience. Iterate based on the results to continuously improve your approach.

5. Stay Agile: Trends can change rapidly. Stay agile and be ready to pivot your strategy as new trends emerge. Flexibility is crucial for staying relevant in the fast-paced world of social media.

## Tools for Trend Analysis

1. BuzzSumo: An excellent tool for discovering trending content and influencers. It helps identify the most shared content across social media platforms.

2. Mention: Tracks brand mentions and conversations across social media, providing insights into what's being talked about and trending.

3. Social Mention: A real-time social media search and analysis tool that aggregates user-generated content into a single stream of information.

4. Hashtagify: Helps discover and analyze the most popular hashtags. It's useful for understanding which hashtags are trending and how they relate to each other.

5. Google Alerts: Set up alerts for specific keywords related to your industry. Google Alerts notifies you when new

content is published, keeping you informed of the latest trends.

Analyzing current trends is an essential step in becoming a successful trendsetter. By leveraging tools and strategies to identify and understand trends, you can create content that resonates with your audience and positions you at the forefront of social media innovation. Stay informed, adaptable, and creative to continuously set and lead trends in your niche.

# 4

# Creating Trend-Worthy Content

**Creating Trend-Worthy Content**

Creating content that has the potential to set trends involves a mix of creativity, strategic planning, and a deep understanding of your audience. This chapter will guide you through the essential elements of crafting compelling content that captures attention and encourages sharing.

**Understanding Your Audience**

To create content that resonates, you must first understand who your audience is:

1. Demographics: Know your audience's age, gender, location, and interests.
2. Preferences: Understand what types of content they engage with the most—videos, images, articles, etc.

3. Pain Points and Desires: Identify their challenges and what they aspire to achieve. Content that addresses these areas tends to perform well.
4. Behavior: Monitor their online behavior, such as when they are most active on social media and what platforms they prefer.

## Elements of Trend-Worthy Content

### 1. High-Quality Visuals

Professional Photography and Videography: Invest in good equipment or hire professionals. Clear, high-resolution images and videos are more likely to catch the eye.

Editing and Design: Use tools like Adobe Photoshop, Lightroom, or Canva to enhance your visuals. Consistent branding and aesthetics help create a recognizable style.

### 2. Compelling Storytelling

Narrative Structure: Craft your content with a clear beginning, middle, and end. Good stories engage viewers and encourage them to share.

Authenticity: Authentic content builds trust and relatability. Share real experiences, behind-the-scenes looks, and personal stories.

Emotion: Content that evokes strong emotions—whether it's joy, surprise, or empathy—is more likely to be shared. Use humor, inspirational stories, or heartwarming moments to connect emotionally.

### 3. Relevance and Timeliness

Current Events: Tie your content to current events or trending topics. This makes your content more relevant and increases its chances of being shared.

Seasonal Content: Create content around holidays, seasons, and special occasions. Seasonal content is often more relatable and timely.

Cultural References: Use pop culture references, memes, and internet culture to make your content relatable to a broader audience.

### 4. Innovation and Creativity

Unique Concepts: Bring fresh ideas to the table. Unique and innovative content stands out in the crowded social media landscape.

Interactive Content: Use polls, quizzes, and interactive videos to engage your audience. Interactive content encourages participation and sharing.

Visual Effects and Animations: Incorporate eye-catching visual effects and animations. Tools like After Effects and Premiere Pro can help create stunning visuals.

## 5. Engagement and Call-to-Actions

Ask Questions: Encourage interaction by asking questions in your posts. This invites your audience to engage and share their opinions.

Challenges and Contests: Create challenges or contests that encourage user participation. Use branded hashtags to track entries and increase visibility.

Clear CTAs: Include clear calls-to-action, such as asking viewers to share, comment, or tag friends. Effective CTAs drive engagement and expand your content's reach.

## Platforms and Formats

1. Facebook

Videos and Live Streams: Video content tends to perform well on Facebook. Use live streams for real-time engagement.

Stories: Utilize Facebook Stories for short, engaging updates.

Group Posts: Engage with niche communities through Facebook Groups.

2. Instagram

Reels and Stories: Use Reels for short, engaging videos and Stories for daily updates and behind-the-scenes content.

IGTV: Create longer videos for in-depth content.

High-Quality Photos: Maintain a visually appealing feed with high-quality images.

3. Twitter

Concise Tweets: Craft short, witty, and engaging tweets.

Threads: Use threads to provide more detailed information.

Real-Time Updates: Engage in real-time conversations around trending topics.

4. TikTok

Short-Form Videos: Focus on creativity and authenticity in your short videos.

Challenges: Participate in and create your own challenges.

Trending Sounds: Use popular sounds and music to increase discoverability.

5. YouTube

Long-Form Videos: Create comprehensive and high-quality videos.

SEO Optimization: Optimize your video titles, descriptions, and tags for better search visibility.

Engaging Thumbnails: Design eye-catching thumbnails to attract clicks.

6. LinkedIn

Professional Insights: Share industry insights, case studies, and professional advice.

Long-Form Articles: Publish articles to establish thought leadership.

Network Engagement: Engage with your professional network through comments and shares.

## Tools for Content Creation

1. Canva: For designing graphics and visuals.
2. Adobe Creative Suite: For professional photo and video editing.
3. Final Cut Pro: For video editing.
4. Loom: For creating and sharing quick video messages.
5. Animoto: For creating professional videos easily.
6. Buffer: For scheduling and managing social media posts.

7. Hootsuite: For social media management and analytics.

Creating trend-worthy content involves a blend of creativity, strategic thinking, and audience understanding. By focusing on high-quality visuals, compelling storytelling, relevance, and innovation, you can craft content that not only captures attention but also encourages sharing and engagement. Tailor your content to fit the strengths of each platform and continuously experiment with new ideas to stay ahead of the curve.

# 5

# Leveraging Influencers and Partnerships

**Leveraging Influencers and Partnerships**

In the world of social media, influencers and partnerships can significantly amplify your reach and impact. This chapter explores how to effectively collaborate with influencers and other brands to set trends and enhance your social media presence.

## Understanding Influencers

Influencers are individuals with a substantial following and the ability to sway their audience's opinions and behaviors. They can be categorized into several types:

1. Mega-Influencers: Celebrities and public figures with millions of followers.

2. Macro-Influencers: Established influencers with hundreds of thousands to millions of followers.

3. Micro-Influencers: Influencers with 10,000 to 100,000 followers, often with highly engaged audiences.

4. Nano-Influencers: Everyday individuals with 1,000 to 10,000 followers, known for their close-knit communities.

## Benefits of Influencer Collaborations

1. Extended Reach: Influencers can introduce your brand to their followers, significantly expanding your audience.

2. Credibility and Trust: Influencers have built trust with their audience. A recommendation from them can enhance your brand's credibility.

3. Engagement: Influencers often have high engagement rates. Their content can generate more likes, comments, and shares.

4. Content Creation: Influencers can create unique and high-quality content for your brand, providing fresh perspectives.

## Finding the Right Influencers

1. Identify Your Goals: Define what you want to achieve with influencer collaborations—brand awareness, engagement, sales, etc.

2. Research Influencers: Use tools like BuzzSumo, HypeAuditor, and Influencity to find influencers who align with your brand values and audience.

3. Analyze Engagement: Look beyond follower count. Assess engagement rates, audience demographics, and content quality.

4. Check Authenticity: Ensure the influencer's followers are genuine and their engagement is organic. Tools like Social Blade can help analyze follower growth patterns.

## Building Relationships with Influencers

1. Personalized Outreach: Reach out with personalized messages that show you've done your homework and genuinely admire their work.

2. Offer Value: Clearly outline what you're offering in return, whether it's monetary compensation, free products, or exclusive experiences.

3. Be Transparent: Discuss expectations, deliverables, timelines, and compensation upfront. Transparency builds trust and sets a professional tone.

4. Long-Term Partnerships: Consider building long-term relationships with influencers rather than one-off campaigns. This can lead to more authentic and impactful collaborations.

## Effective Collaboration Strategies

1. Co-Creation: Involve influencers in the creative process. Co-created content feels more authentic and resonates better with their audience.

2. Takeovers: Allow influencers to take over your social media accounts for a day. This provides a fresh perspective and attracts their followers to your platform.

3. Giveaways and Contests: Partner with influencers to host giveaways and contests. This can drive engagement and attract new followers.

4. Events and Live Streams: Collaborate on live events, webinars, or live streams. Real-time interactions can boost engagement and excitement.

## Leveraging Brand Partnerships

1. Identify Complementary Brands: Partner with brands that share your values and have a similar target audience but are not direct competitors.

2. Joint Campaigns: Collaborate on joint marketing campaigns, such as co-branded content, shared promotions, or cross-promotions.

3. Product Collaborations: Develop co-branded products or limited edition items. This can generate buzz and attract fans of both brands.

4. Event Sponsorships: Co-sponsor events or host joint events to increase visibility and engage with a broader audience.

## Measuring Success

1. Track Metrics: Monitor key performance indicators (KPIs) such as reach, engagement, website traffic, and conversions.

2. Analyze ROI: Calculate the return on investment (ROI) by comparing the cost of the collaboration with the value generated (e.g., sales, new followers, brand awareness).

3. Gather Feedback: Collect feedback from the influencer and their audience to understand what worked well and what could be improved.

4. Adjust Strategies: Use insights from your analysis to refine your approach for future collaborations.

## Tools for Influencer and Partnership Management

1. Influencity: For finding and managing influencer collaborations.

2. BuzzSumo: To identify popular influencers and track content performance.

3. Hootsuite: For scheduling and monitoring social media campaigns.

4. Traackr: For managing influencer relationships and measuring impact.

5. Google Analytics: To track website traffic and conversions from influencer campaigns.

Leveraging influencers and partnerships can significantly enhance your social media strategy. By carefully selecting the right collaborators, building strong relationships, and executing strategic campaigns, you can amplify your reach, build credibility, and set impactful trends. Continuously measure your success and refine your approach to stay ahead in the dynamic world of social media.

# 6

# Utilizing Hashtags and Trends

**Utilizing Hashtags and Trends**

Hashtags and trends are powerful tools on social media that can significantly boost your content's visibility and engagement. This chapter explores how to effectively use hashtags and participate in trends to amplify your reach and set trends.

**Understanding Hashtags**

Hashtags are keywords or phrases preceded by the # symbol. They categorize content and make it discoverable to a broader audience. By using relevant hashtags, you can tap into existing conversations and attract users interested in specific topics.

## Types of Hashtags

1. Branded Hashtags: Unique to your brand, these can be your company name, tagline, or campaign-specific. They help in building brand identity and encouraging user-generated content.

2. Community Hashtags: Used by a specific group or community, these help connect like-minded individuals. Examples include #Foodie for food enthusiasts or #FitnessGoals for fitness communities.

3. Trending Hashtags: These are currently popular and can provide a quick boost in visibility. They are often related to current events, holidays, or viral topics.

4. Content Hashtags: Related to the content you're posting, such as #TravelPhotography for travel photos or #DIYProjects for DIY content.

5. Event Hashtags: Used for specific events, such as #SXSW for South by Southwest or #Olympics for the Olympic Games.

## Finding the Right Hashtags

1. Research Tools: Use tools like Hashtagify, RiteTag, and Tagboard to discover popular and relevant hashtags.

2. Competitor Analysis: Observe the hashtags your competitors are using successfully.

3. Trending Sections: Check the trending sections on Twitter, Instagram, and other platforms to find popular hashtags.

4. Engage with Your Audience: Pay attention to the hashtags your audience is using and engaging with.

**Best Practices for Using Hashtags**

1. Relevance: Ensure your hashtags are relevant to your content and audience. Irrelevant hashtags can appear spammy.

2. Optimal Number: Use a mix of popular and niche hashtags. While Instagram allows up to 30 hashtags, the optimal number can be around 10-15. On Twitter, 1-2 hashtags per tweet are recommended.

3. Placement: Place hashtags in the caption for Instagram or at the end of your tweet or post for other platforms. Avoid overloading your content with hashtags.

4. Branded Hashtags: Create and promote your own branded hashtags. Encourage your audience to use them in their posts.

5. Engage with Hashtags: Actively engage with posts under the hashtags you use. Like, comment, and share relevant content to build community.

## Participating in Trends

1. Stay Updated: Follow current events, pop culture, and industry news to stay aware of emerging trends.

2. Quick Response: Act quickly to participate in trends. Timing is crucial as trends can change rapidly.

3. Creative Twist: Add your unique spin to trends. Originality and creativity can make your content stand out.

4. Consistency: Regularly participate in trends that align with your brand. Consistency helps in building recognition.

5. User-Generated Content: Encourage your audience to participate in trends and share their content using your branded hashtags.

## Creating Your Own Trends

1. Identify Gaps: Look for gaps in current trends and identify opportunities for new ideas.

2. Innovative Ideas: Develop unique and innovative ideas that resonate with your audience. This be a new challenge, hashtag, or content format.

3. Collaborate: Partner with influencers, other brands, and your audience to amplify your trend. Collaborations can provide the initial push needed for a trend to take off.

4. Promotion: Use all available channels to promote your trend. This includes social media platforms, email newsletters, and even offline events.

5. Engagement: Actively engage with participants in your trend. Acknowledge their contributions and encourage ongoing participation.

## Case Studies

1. #IceBucketChallenge: This viral challenge raised awareness and funds for ALS. It involved people dumping ice water over their heads and nominating others to do the same. The simplicity and social aspect contributed to its massive success.

2. #ShareACoke: Coca-Cola's campaign involved personalized Coke bottles with popular names. It encouraged people to find bottles with their names and share photos on social media, significantly boosting engagement and sales.

3. #InMyFeelingsChallenge: Originating from a viral dance to Drake's song, this challenge spread quickly with celebrities and influencers participating, demonstrating the power of music and dance trends on platforms like TikTok and Instagram.

## Tools for Managing Hashtags and Trends

1. Hashtagify: For discovering popular hashtags and analyzing their performance.

2. RiteTag: Provides instant hashtag suggestions based on your image and text.

3. Tagboard: Aggregates content from different platforms based on hashtags.

4. Trendsmap: Visualizes trending hashtags and topics in real-time.

5. Sprout Social: Offers social media management and analytics, including hashtag performance tracking.

Effectively utilizing hashtags and participating in trends can greatly enhance your social media strategy. By staying relevant, engaging with your audience, and creatively participating in or creating trends, you can significantly boost your visibility and influence on social media. Consistent and strategic use of hashtags and trends will position you as a proactive and innovative presence in the social media landscape.

# 7

# Engaging with Your Audience

**Engaging with Your Audience**

Engaging with your audience is a critical component of setting trends and building a strong social media presence. This chapter explores the importance of audience engagement, strategies for fostering interaction, and tools to facilitate effective communication.

**The Importance of Engagement**

1. Builds Community: Engagement fosters a sense of community and belonging among your audience.

2. Increases Visibility: Social media algorithms often prioritize content with high engagement, increasing your reach.

3. Enhances Loyalty: Active engagement builds trust and loyalty, encouraging followers to become brand advocates.

4. Provides Insights: Interaction with your audience offers valuable feedback and insights into their preferences and behaviors.

5. Drives Action: Engaged audiences are more likely to take desired actions, such as making a purchase, sharing content, or participating in campaigns.

## Strategies for Effective Engagement

1. Respond Promptly: Respond to comments, messages, and mentions in a timely manner. Prompt responses show that you value your audience's input.

2. Ask Questions: Encourage interaction by asking open-ended questions in your posts. This invites followers to share their thoughts and experiences.

3. Host Q&A Sessions: Conduct live Q&A sessions on platforms like Instagram Live, Facebook Live, or Twitter Spaces to engage directly with your audience.

4. User-Generated Content: Encourage followers to create and share content related to your brand. Reposting user-generated content shows appreciation and fosters community.

5. Interactive Content: Use polls, quizzes, and interactive stories to engage your audience. Platforms like Instagram and Twitter offer built-in tools for this.

6. Personalization: Address followers by their names and personalize responses to make interactions feel more genuine and meaningful.

7. Celebrate Milestones: Acknowledge and celebrate milestones such as follower count achievements, anniversaries, and community accomplishments.

### Creating a Two-Way Conversation

1. Listen Actively: Pay attention to what your audience is saying about your brand and industry. Use social listening tools to monitor conversations.

2. Encourage Feedback: Regularly ask for feedback on products, services, and content. Constructive feedback helps you improve and shows that you value your audience's opinions.

3. Acknowledge Contributions: Highlight and thank followers who actively engage with your content. This can be done through shoutouts, features, or special rewards.

4. Transparency and Authenticity: Be open and honest in your communications. Authenticity builds trust and encourages more meaningful interactions.

5. Handle Criticism Gracefully: Address negative feedback and criticism constructively. Show that you're listening and willing to make improvements.

## Engaging Through Different Content Formats

1. Videos and Live Streams: Videos and live streams offer a dynamic way to engage with your audience. Live interactions create a real-time connection.

2. Stories and Reels: Use Instagram Stories, Facebook Stories, and TikTok Reels to share behind-the-scenes content, updates, and quick polls.

3. Infographics and Visuals: Create visually appealing infographics and graphics that are easy to share and understand.

4. Blogs and Articles: Share in-depth articles and blog posts that provide value to your audience. Encourage comments and discussions around the content.

5. Podcasts and Audio Content: Start a podcast or share audio content that delves into topics of interest to your audience. Invite listeners to submit questions and topics.

## Measuring Engagement

1. Engagement Rate: Calculate the engagement rate by dividing the total engagement (likes, comments, shares) by the total number of followers and multiplying by 100.

2. Comments and Replies: Track the number of comments and replies on your posts. High numbers indicate active participation.

3. Shares and Retweets: Monitor how often your content is shared or retweeted. This reflects your content's resonance with the audience.

4. Direct Messages: Track the volume and quality of direct messages. Frequent DMs indicate a strong connection with your audience.

5. Story Views and Interactions: Measure the views and interactions on your stories. This provides insights into which content formats engage your audience the most.

## Tools for Audience Engagement

1. Hootsuite: For scheduling posts, monitoring conversations, and engaging with your audience across multiple platforms.

2. Sprout Social: Offers robust engagement tools, including social listening and detailed analytics.

3. Buffer: Provides engagement features and insights to help manage and respond to interactions.

4. AgoraPulse: Offers social media management tools with a focus on engagement and community building.

5. SocialBee: Helps schedule and manage posts while also tracking and analyzing engagement.

Engaging with your audience is essential for building a loyal and active community on social media. By employing effective engagement strategies, creating interactive content, and using the right tools, you can foster meaningful interactions that not only enhance your social media presence but also set the stage for trendsetting. Remember, engagement is a two-way street—listen, respond, and create a dialogue that keeps your audience coming back for more.

# 8

# Analyzing and Adapting Your Strategy

**Analyzing and Adapting Your Strategy**

Continuous analysis and adaptation of your social media strategy are crucial for staying relevant and effective in the ever-changing social media landscape. This chapter will guide you through the process of analyzing your performance, identifying areas for improvement, and adapting your strategy to achieve better results.

### The Importance of Analytics

1. Informed Decision Making: Analytics provide data-driven insights that inform your strategic decisions.

2. Measuring Success: Track your progress towards goals and assess the effectiveness of your campaigns.

3. Identifying Trends: Spot emerging trends and adjust your strategy to capitalize on them.

4. Understanding Audience Behavior: Gain insights into your audience's preferences, behaviors, and engagement patterns.

5. Optimizing Content: Determine which types of content perform best and refine your approach accordingly.

## Key Metrics to Track

1. Engagement Metrics

Likes: Indicates initial positive reception of your content.

Comments: Shows deeper engagement and interaction with your posts.

Shares: Reflects content value and willingness to recommend to others.

Mentions: Measures brand visibility and audience advocacy.

2. Reach and Impressions

Reach: The total number of unique users who have seen your content.

Impressions: The total number of times your content is displayed, regardless of clicks.

3. Follower Growth

New Followers: The number of new followers gained over a specific period.

Unfollows: The number of followers lost, indicating possible dissatisfaction.

4. Website Traffic

Referral Traffic: Traffic directed to your website from social media platforms.

Click-Through Rate (CTR): The percentage of users who click on a link in your post.

5. Conversion Metrics

Leads Generated: The number of potential customers acquired through social media.

Sales and Revenue: Direct sales attributed to social media efforts.

Conversion Rate: The percentage of visitors who complete a desired action (e.g., making a purchase).

6. Content Performance

Top-Performing Posts: Identify which posts have the highest engagement and reach.

Least-Performing Posts: Determine which posts underperform and analyze why.

## Tools for Social Media Analytics

1. Google Analytics: Track website traffic and conversions from social media.

2. Hootsuite Analytics: Provides comprehensive insights across multiple platforms.

3. Sprout Social: Offers detailed engagement, reach, and audience analysis.

4. Buffer Analyze: Focuses on performance metrics for posts and stories.

5. Iconosquare: Specializes in Instagram and Facebook analytics.

## Analyzing Your Data

1. Set Clear Objectives: Define what success looks like for your social media strategy (e.g., increased engagement, higher sales, more followers).

2. Collect Data Regularly: Consistently gather data to monitor trends and changes over time.

3. Compare Periods: Analyze data over different periods to identify patterns and seasonal trends.

4. Benchmarking: Compare your performance against industry standards and competitors.

## Adapting Your Strategy

1. Identify Strengths and Weaknesses

Strengths: Leverage high-performing content types, platforms, and tactics.

Weaknesses: Address underperforming areas by experimenting with new approaches.

2. Adjust Content Strategy

Content Types: Focus on formats that generate the most engagement (e.g., videos, infographics, live streams).

Posting Times: Post when your audience is most active to maximize reach and interaction.

3. Refine Audience Targeting

Segmentation: Segment your audience based on demographics, behaviors, and interests to tailor your content.

Personalization: Personalize your messaging to resonate more deeply with different audience segments.

4. Experiment with New Trends

Emerging Platforms: Explore new social media platforms and features.

Trendy Content: Create content that taps into current trends and challenges.

5. Optimize Campaigns

A/B Testing: Test different versions of ads, posts, and calls-to-action to determine what works best.

Budget Allocation: Allocate more budget to high-performing campaigns and reduce spending on less effective ones.

6. Continuous Learning

Stay Informed: Keep up with the latest social media trends, tools, and best practices.

Feedback Loop: Use audience feedback and analytics insights to continuously improve your strategy.

Analyzing and adapting your social media strategy is an ongoing process that requires vigilance, flexibility, and a data-driven approach. By regularly monitoring your performance, understanding your audience, and being willing to experiment and innovate, you can maintain a dynamic and effective social media presence. This continuous cycle of analysis and adaptation will ensure that your strategy remains relevant and impactful, helping you to set and sustain trends in the ever-evolving social media landscape.

# 9

# Creating Viral Content

**Creating Viral Content**

Creating content that goes viral is often seen as the holy grail of social media strategy. While there's no guaranteed formula for virality, certain principles and techniques can increase your chances of producing highly shareable content. This chapter explores the elements that contribute to virality and offers practical tips for creating content that captures the attention and imagination of a broad audience.

**Understanding Virality**

Virality occurs when content rapidly spreads across social media platforms, reaching a wide audience in a short period. This can happen organically or through strategic promotion. Viral content often elicits strong emotional responses, encourages interaction, and prompts users to share it with their networks.

## Key Elements of Viral Content

1. Emotional Appeal

Humor: Funny content is highly shareable because it brings joy and laughter.

Inspiration: Stories of triumph, resilience, and kindness resonate deeply with audiences.

Surprise: Unexpected or shocking content captures attention and prompts shares.

Relatability: Content that reflects common experiences or feelings encourages users to share their own stories.

2. Engagement Triggers

Calls to Action: Encourage viewers to like, comment, share, or participate in a challenge.

Interactive Elements: Quizzes, polls, and challenges increase engagement and shareability.

Questions: Ask thought-provoking questions that invite responses and discussions.

3. Visual Appeal

High-Quality Images and Videos: Visually appealing content stands out in crowded feeds.

Eye-Catching Thumbnails: Attractive thumbnails increase the likelihood of clicks and shares.

Memes and GIFs: Easily digestible and entertaining visual formats that are highly shareable.

4. Relevance and Timeliness

Current Events: Content that ties into trending news, holidays, or cultural events is more likely to be shared.

Pop Culture: References to popular movies, TV shows, music, or celebrities can boost engagement.

Seasonal Content: Tailor content to align with seasons, holidays, or significant events.

## Steps to Create Viral Content

1. Know Your Audience

Demographics: Understand the age, gender, location, and interests of your target audience.

Psychographics: Identify the values, attitudes, and lifestyle choices of your audience.

Behavior: Analyze how your audience interacts with content—what they like, share, and comment on.

2. Craft a Compelling Story

Strong Narrative: Develop a clear and engaging story arc with a beginning, middle, and end.

Emotional Hook: Start with an element that captures attention and evokes an emotional response.

Relatable Characters: Use characters or personas that your audience can relate to or aspire to.

### 3. Optimize for Platforms

Platform-Specific Content: Tailor your content to fit the format and style of each social media platform.

Length and Format: Adjust the length of videos, captions, and posts to suit platform preferences.

Use Hashtags: Include relevant hashtags to increase discoverability and engagement.

### 4. Leverage Influencers

Collaborations: Partner with influencers who can amplify your content to their followers.

Challenges and Contests: Create challenges or contests that influencers can participate in and promote.

### 5. Encourage User Participation

User-Generated Content: Invite your audience to create and share their own content related to your campaign.

Challenges: Launch challenges that prompt users to perform specific actions and share their results.

Contests: Run contests that reward users for sharing your content or creating their own.

6. Promote and Distribute

Paid Promotion: Use social media ads to boost visibility and reach a broader audience.

Cross-Promotion: Share your content across multiple platforms and encourage partners to do the same.

Email Marketing: Include viral content in your email newsletters to reach your subscribers.

**Case Studies**

1. ALS Ice Bucket Challenge: This viral campaign involved people dumping ice water over their heads and nominating others to do the same, raising awareness and funds for ALS.

The combination of a clear call to action, participation of celebrities, and emotional appeal contributed to its success.

2. Dove's Real Beauty Sketches: This campaign featured an artist drawing women based on their self-descriptions and descriptions from strangers. The contrast highlighted issues of self-esteem and body image, resonating deeply with viewers and encouraging shares.

3. Old Spice's "The Man Your Man Could Smell Like": Old Spice's humorous and surprising videos, featuring the charismatic character played by Isaiah Mustafa, were highly shareable and generated significant buzz across social media.

## Tools for Creating Viral Content

1. Canva: For creating visually appealing graphics and social media posts.

2. Adobe Spark: For designing high-quality visuals and videos.

3. BuzzSumo: To identify trending topics and analyze what content is performing well.

4. Animoto: For creating engaging videos quickly and easily.

5. Hootsuite: For scheduling and promoting content across multiple social media platforms.

Creating viral content is both an art and a science, requiring creativity, strategic planning, and a deep understanding of your audience. By focusing on emotional appeal, engagement triggers, visual appeal, and relevance, you can increase your chances of producing content that resonates widely and is shared extensively. Remember, while virality can't be guaranteed, consistently applying these principles and learning from your successes and failures will enhance your ability to create impactful and shareable content.

# 10

# Leveraging Influencers and Partnerships

**Leveraging Influencers and Partnerships**

Influencers and partnerships can play a crucial role in amplifying your social media presence and setting trends. This chapter explores how to identify the right influencers, build effective partnerships, and leverage these relationships to enhance your social media strategy.

**Understanding Influencer Marketing**

Influencer marketing involves collaborating with individuals who have a significant and engaged following on social media. These influencers can help you reach a broader audience, build credibility, and drive engagement with your brand.

## Types of Influencers

1. Mega-Influencers: Celebrities and public figures with millions of followers. They offer massive reach but may lack niche-specific engagement.

2. Macro-Influencers: Individuals with hundreds of thousands to millions of followers. They balance reach and engagement.

3. Micro-Influencers: Individuals with 10,000 to 100,000 followers. They often have high engagement rates and a strong connection with their audience.

4. Nano-Influencers: Individuals with fewer than 10,000 followers. They have very high engagement and a personal touch with their followers.

## Identifying the Right Influencers

1. Relevance: Ensure the influencer's content aligns with your brand values, industry, and target audience.

2. Engagement: Look for influencers with high engagement rates rather than just large followings.

3. Authenticity: Choose influencers who genuinely connect with their audience and maintain authenticity in their content.

4. Reach: Consider the influencer's reach within your target market.

5. Past Collaborations: Review their previous collaborations to understand their professionalism and the outcomes of those partnerships.

## Building Effective Partnerships

1. Research and Vetting

Analyze Content: Review the influencer's content quality, style, and audience interactions.

Check Metrics: Use tools like Social Blade, HypeAuditor, or Influencer.co to verify their follower count, engagement rates, and growth trends.

Engagement Authenticity: Ensure their engagement is genuine, not artificially inflated by bots or fake followers.

2. Establish Clear Objectives

Goals: Define what you aim to achieve from the partnership (e.g., brand awareness, product launches, driving traffic).

KPIs: Set Key Performance Indicators to measure the success of the collaboration.

### 3. Outreach and Negotiation

Personalized Outreach: Craft personalized messages that highlight why you believe they are a perfect fit for your brand.

Value Proposition: Clearly state the benefits of the partnership for the influencer.

Negotiation: Discuss terms, compensation, and deliverables. Be clear about expectations and timelines.

### 4. Collaborative Planning

Content Strategy: Work with the influencer to develop a content strategy that aligns with both your brand and their style.

Creative Freedom: Allow the influencer some creative freedom to maintain authenticity.

Timeline: Establish a clear timeline for content creation, approval, and posting.

5. Execution and Monitoring

Content Approval: Review and approve content before it goes live to ensure brand alignment.

Monitor Performance: Track the performance of the posts using analytics tools to measure engagement, reach, and conversions.

Engage with Content: Actively engage with the content by liking, commenting, and sharing to show support and amplify reach.

6. Review and Optimize

Analyze Results: Evaluate the success of the campaign against your KPIs.

Feedback Loop: Provide and request feedback to understand what worked and what can be improved.

Long-Term Relationships: Build long-term relationships with successful influencers for ongoing collaborations.

## Leveraging Partnerships

1. Brand Collaborations

Co-Branding: Partner with complementary brands to create joint campaigns that benefit both parties.

Shared Audiences: Tap into each other's audiences for increased reach and engagement.

2. User-Generated Content (UGC)

Encourage UGC: Motivate your audience to create and share content related to your brand.

Feature UGC: Share user-generated content on your platforms to build community and trust.

3. Affiliate Programs

Incentivize Partnerships: Create affiliate programs where influencers earn commissions for driving sales or leads.

Track Performance: Use tracking links and codes to monitor the performance of affiliate partners.

4. Event Collaborations

Host Joint Events: Partner with influencers for live events, webinars, or virtual meetups.

Event Coverage: Collaborate with influencers to cover events and provide behind-the-scenes content.

## Case Studies

1. Daniel Wellington: The watch brand used micro-influencers to build brand awareness and drive sales. By providing influencers with watches to showcase, they created a massive social media presence.

2. Fiji Water: Partnered with influencers at high-profile events like the Golden Globes, resulting in viral moments and increased brand visibility.

3. Glossier: Utilized a combination of micro-influencers and customer ambassadors to create authentic and relatable content, driving significant brand growth and loyalty.

**Tools for Influencer Marketing**

1. BuzzSumo: To identify influencers and analyze their content performance.

2. HypeAuditor: For in-depth influencer analytics and audience insights.

3. Influence.co: A platform for finding and connecting with influencers.

4. Upfluence: An all-in-one influencer marketing platform for managing campaigns.

5. AspireIQ: To build and manage influencer relationships and campaigns.

Leveraging influencers and partnerships can significantly enhance your social media strategy by expanding your reach, increasing engagement, and building credibility. By carefully selecting the right influencers, establishing clear objectives, and fostering collaborative relationships, you can create impactful campaigns that resonate with your audience and set trends. Remember, the key to successful influencer marketing lies in authenticity, strategic planning, and continuous optimization.

# 11

# Harnessing the Power of Paid Advertising

**Harnessing the Power of Paid Advertising**

While organic growth is vital for long-term success, paid advertising can significantly boost your reach and accelerate trendsetting on social media. This chapter delves into the nuances of paid advertising, including strategies, platforms, budgeting, and measuring success.

**Understanding Paid Advertising**

Paid advertising involves paying social media platforms to promote your content, reach a larger audience, and achieve specific marketing goals. This can include increased visibility, website traffic, lead generation, and sales.

## Benefits Of Paid Advertisement

1. Increased Reach: Paid ads can reach a broader and more targeted audience than organic posts.

2. Faster Results: Paid campaigns can quickly boost visibility and engagement.

3. Precise Targeting: Advanced targeting options allow you to reach specific demographics, interests, and behaviors.

4. Measurable ROI: Detailed analytics help track performance and measure return on investment.

5. Enhanced Brand Awareness: Consistent ad presence can strengthen brand recognition and recall.

## Key Platforms for Paid Advertising

1. Facebook Ads

Audience Network: Extend reach beyond Facebook to partner apps and websites.

Targeting Options: Demographics, interests, behaviors, and custom audiences.

Ad Formats: Image, video, carousel, slideshow, collection, and instant experience ads.

2. Instagram Ads

Visual Appeal: Leverage high-quality visuals to engage the audience.

Stories Ads: Full-screen ads in Stories for immersive experiences.

Shopping Ads: Direct users to purchase products directly from the platform.

3. Twitter Ads

Promoted Tweets: Boost the reach of specific tweets.

Follower Campaigns: Increase followers to build your audience.

Trend Takeovers: Promote your hashtag or trend at the top of trending topics.

4. LinkedIn Ads

Professional Audience: Target professionals based on job title, industry, and company size.

Sponsored Content: Promote posts in the LinkedIn feed.

InMail: Send personalized messages directly to users' inboxes.

5. YouTube Ads

Video Ads: Pre-roll, mid-roll, and post-roll ads within videos.

TrueView Ads: Pay only when users watch the ad for a certain duration.

Display Ads: Banner ads on the YouTube platform.

6. TikTok Ads

In-Feed Ads: Native ads appearing in users' feed.

Branded Hashtag Challenges: Encourage user-generated content around a branded hashtag.

Branded Effects: Custom filters and effects for users to apply in their videos.

**Crafting Effective Paid Campaigns**

1. Set Clear Objectives

Awareness: Increase brand visibility and reach.

Consideration: Drive traffic to your website or landing page.

Conversion: Generate leads, sales, or specific actions.

2. Define Your Target Audience

Demographics: Age, gender, location, language.

Interests and Behaviors: Hobbies, purchasing behavior, online activity.

Custom Audiences: Use customer data to target existing customers or similar audiences.

Lookalike Audiences: Reach new users similar to your best customers.

3. Create Compelling Ad Creative

Visuals: Use high-quality images and videos that grab attention.

Copy: Write clear, concise, and compelling ad copy with a strong call to action (CTA).

A/B Testing: Test different versions of your ad creative to see what performs best.

4. Optimize Landing Pages

Relevance: Ensure the landing page matches the ad's message and CTA.

User Experience: Provide a seamless and easy-to-navigate experience.

Conversion Elements: Include clear CTAs, forms, and purchase options.

## 5. Budgeting and Bidding

Budget Allocation: Decide on daily or lifetime budgets for your campaigns.

Bidding Strategies: Choose between manual and automatic bidding based on your goals (e.g., cost-per-click, cost-per-impression, cost-per-conversion).

Ad Scheduling: Run ads at times when your target audience is most active.

## 6. Monitoring and Optimization

Analytics Tools: Use platform analytics and third-party tools to track performance.

Key Metrics: Monitor metrics such as CTR, conversion rate, cost per conversion, and ROI.

Adjust and Optimize: Continuously refine targeting, ad creative, and bidding strategies based on performance data.

## Advanced Strategies

1. Retargeting Campaigns

Website Visitors: Target users who have visited your website but didn't convert.

Engagement Retargeting: Target users who have interacted with your social media posts or ads.

Email Retargeting: Use email lists to retarget existing customers or leads.

2. Lookalike Audiences

Expand Reach: Use data from your best-performing audiences to find new, similar users.

Segmentation: Create multiple lookalike audiences based on different customer segments.

3. Dynamic Ads

Personalization: Serve personalized ads based on user behavior and interests.

Product Catalog Ads: Automatically show relevant products to users based on their browsing history.

4. Cross-Platform Campaigns

Integrated Approach: Run coordinated campaigns across multiple platforms for consistent messaging.

Sequential Messaging: Deliver a sequence of ads to guide users through the customer journey.

**Case Studies**

1. Airbnb: Leveraged Facebook and Instagram ads with stunning visuals and targeted audiences to increase bookings and brand awareness.

2.Dollar Shave Club: Used humorous and relatable video ads on YouTube and Facebook to quickly grow their customer base.

3. Shopify: Implemented LinkedIn ads targeting entrepreneurs and small business owners, driving significant traffic and conversions.

## Tools for Managing Paid Advertising

1. Facebook Ads Manager: Comprehensive tool for creating, managing, and analyzing Facebook and Instagram ads.

2. Google Ads: Platform for managing ads across Google Search, YouTube, and the Google Display Network.

3. AdEspresso: Helps create, manage, and optimize Facebook and Instagram ads.

4. Hootsuite Ads: Integrates with Hootsuite for managing ads across multiple platforms.

5. WordStream: Provides tools for optimizing Google Ads, Bing Ads, and Facebook Ads.

Paid advertising is a powerful tool to enhance your social media strategy, accelerate growth, and set trends. By understanding the benefits, choosing the right platforms, crafting effective campaigns, and continuously optimizing your efforts, you can achieve significant results. Combining organic efforts with strategic paid advertising will help you maximize your reach, engagement, and conversions, ensuring a robust and impactful social media presence.

# 12

# Building a Community and Engaging with Your Audience

## Building a Community and Engaging with Your Audience

Creating a loyal and engaged community around your brand is vital for sustained success on social media. This chapter delves into strategies for building a vibrant community, fostering meaningful interactions, and maintaining long-term engagement with your audience.

### The Importance of Community Building

1. Brand Loyalty: An engaged community develops a deeper connection with your brand, leading to increased loyalty and repeat business.

2. Trust and Credibility: Active engagement and positive interactions build trust and establish your brand as credible and reliable.

3. User-Generated Content: Community members are more likely to create and share content related to your brand, amplifying your reach.

4. Customer Insights: Engaging with your audience provides valuable feedback and insights into their needs, preferences, and pain points.

5. Organic Growth: A strong community can drive organic growth through word-of-mouth and social sharing.

## Strategies for Building a Community

1. Define Your Community Goals

Purpose: Clearly define the purpose and goals of your community (e.g., support, education, engagement).

Objectives: Set specific, measurable objectives to track your progress (e.g., increase engagement by 20%, grow community size by 1,000 members).

2. Choose the Right Platforms

Facebook Groups: Ideal for building communities around shared interests and facilitating discussions.

Reddit: Suitable for niche communities and in-depth discussions.

Discord: Great for real-time communication and creating a sense of belonging.

LinkedIn Groups: Best for professional and industry-specific communities.

Instagram: Use hashtags and stories to create a sense of community.

3. Create Valuable Content

Educational Content: Provide informative and educational content that addresses your audience's needs and interests.

Entertaining Content: Share entertaining and engaging content to foster a sense of fun and connection.

Exclusive Content: Offer exclusive content, such as behind-the-scenes looks, early access to products, or special discounts, to reward your community members.

4. Encourage Interaction and Participation

Ask Questions: Prompt discussions by asking open-ended questions.

Polls and Surveys: Use polls and surveys to gather opinions and feedback.

Challenges and Contests: Organize challenges and contests to encourage participation and creativity.

Feature Members: Highlight community members' contributions and achievements.

5. Foster a Positive Environment

Set Guidelines: Establish clear community guidelines to ensure respectful and constructive interactions.

Moderate Effectively: Actively moderate discussions to prevent negativity and maintain a positive atmosphere.

Acknowledge Contributions: Recognize and appreciate members' contributions to foster a sense of belonging.

## Engaging with Your Audience

1. Be Responsive

Timely Replies: Respond to comments, messages, and mentions promptly.

Personalized Responses: Personalize your responses to make your audience feel valued and heard.

Follow Up: Follow up on questions or issues to ensure they are resolved satisfactorily.

2. Humanize Your Brand

Show Personality: Let your brand's personality shine through in your interactions.

Share Behind-the-Scenes: Give your audience a glimpse behind the scenes to create a more personal connection.

Use Humor: Appropriately use humor to make your interactions more relatable and enjoyable.

3. Encourage User-Generated Content (UGC)

Campaigns and Hashtags: Create campaigns and branded hashtags to encourage users to share their content.

UGC Contests: Organize contests that prompt users to create and share content related to your brand.

Feature UGC: Regularly feature user-generated content on your social media channels to recognize and celebrate your community.

4. Host Live Events and Q&A Sessions

Live Streams: Host live streams to interact with your audience in real-time.

Q&A Sessions: Conduct Q&A sessions to address questions and engage with your audience directly.

Webinars and Workshops: Offer webinars and workshops to provide value and foster engagement.

5. Build Relationships with Key Community Members

Identify Influencers: Identify and build relationships with influential community members.

Ambassador Programs: Create ambassador programs to recognize and reward active and loyal members.

Exclusive Access: Provide key members with exclusive access to events, products, or information.

## Measuring Community Engagement

1. Engagement Metrics

Likes, Comments, and Shares: Track the volume and quality of interactions with your content.

Mentions and Tags: Monitor how often your brand is mentioned or tagged by community members.

Active Members: Measure the number of active participants in your community.

2. Growth Metrics

New Members: Track the growth of your community over time.

Retention Rate: Measure how well you retain community members.

3. Sentiment Analysis

Positive vs. Negative Sentiment: Analyze the overall sentiment of interactions to gauge the health of your community.

Feedback and Reviews: Pay attention to feedback and reviews to understand community perceptions.

4. Content Performance

Top-Performing Content: Identify the content that generates the most engagement and interaction.

Content Types: Analyze which types of content resonate most with your community.

## Case Studies

1. LEGO Ideas: LEGO created a platform where fans can submit their own designs, vote on others' ideas, and engage with the brand. This has fostered a highly engaged community and led to new product ideas.

2. Sephora Beauty Insider Community: Sephora's community platform allows beauty enthusiasts to share tips, ask questions, and connect with other fans, enhancing customer loyalty and engagement.

3. Peloton: Peloton has built a strong community around its fitness products by encouraging members to connect, share their workouts, and support each other through social media and the Peloton app.

**Tools for Community Management**

1. Hootsuite: Manage and schedule social media posts, monitor engagement, and analyze performance.

2. Sprout Social: Comprehensive social media management tool with features for engagement, monitoring, and analytics.

3. Discord: Create and manage real-time community chat servers.

4. Mighty Networks: Build and manage your own branded community platform.

5. Facebook Groups: Facilitate community building and engagement directly on Facebook.

**Conclusion**

Building and engaging a community around your brand is essential for long-term social media success. By fostering meaningful interactions, creating valuable content, and actively engaging with your audience, you can create a loyal and vibrant community. Remember, the key to successful community building is consistency, authenticity, and a genuine commitment to your audience's needs and interests. By nurturing your community, you can drive organic growth, enhance brand loyalty, and set trends in the social media landscape.

**All Rights Reserved**
**Fredrick Wonders**
**2024**

www.ingramcontent.com/pod-product-compliance
Lightning Source LLC
Chambersburg PA
CBHW071938210526
45479CB00002B/732